RAD DAD JOKES

SO GOSH DARN FUNNY YOUR SOCKS WILL FALL DOWN

This book is a work of humor and intended to make you laugh and chuckle.

Exterior Cover: Kristy MacDonald

Copyright © 2022 Venti Vinny.

All rights reserved. No part of this publication may be reproduced in any form or by any electronic or mechanical means including information storage and retrieval systems or transmitted in any form or by any means – electronic, mechanical, photocopy, recording, scanning, or other – except for brief quotations in critical reviews or articles, without the prior written permission of the author and copyright owner.

International rights and foreign translations available only through negotiation with the author and copyright owner.

ISBN: 9798837615399

Printed in the United States of America.

TO: _____

FROM: _____

DEDICATION

Thanks so much to YOU amazing men out there!
You know who you are.
wink

INTRODUCTION

What's more amusing than watching your dad repeat the same ole jokes year after year and watch the room squirm uncomfortably because they are just that bad...or good? You've heard that joke so many times you can repeat it word for word.

Who doesn't love Dad jokes?!? We definitely love our dad for telling punny one-liners and making him think he has quite the gift of gab...and jab. Gift your dad the ultimate book to polish up his storyteller skills and have the room in tears – because they can't take it anymore!

This collection will get Dad's creative juices flowing and he'll love these corny, off the wall puns and riddles. So, sit back and watch him take immense pleasure in seeing people laugh (and groan) from the blatant simplicity of a few crafty words.

You look at him, sigh, and all you can say is, "That's <u>MY</u> Dad?"

DEFINITIONS

An unoriginal or unfunny joke of a type supposedly told by middle-aged or older men.[1]

A dad joke is a short joke, typically a pun, presented as a one-liner or a question and answer, but not a narrative. Many dad jokes may be considered anti-jokes, deriving humor from an intentionally not funny punchline.[2]

A wholesome joke of the type said to be told by fathers with a punchline that is often an obvious or predictable pun or play on words and usually judged to be endearingly corny or unfunny.[3]

An indescribably cheesy and/or dumb joke made by a father to his children. A dad joke is when your dad makes extremely corny jokes that are not funny to you, but your friends seem to find them amusing and quite funny. Can sometimes be embarrassing and most of the time laughed at by the dad himself.[4]

---

[1] Google / Oxford Languages
[2] Wikipedia
[3] Merriam-Webster
[4] Urbandictionary.com

RAD DADS SAY...

When does a joke turn into a dad joke? When it becomes apparent.

Why did the golfer bring two pairs of pants? In case he got a hole in one.

What do you call a line of men waiting to get haircuts? A barber queue.

Why do seagulls fly over the sea? If they flew over the bay, they would be bagels.

I'm thinking I should do lunges to stay in shape. That would be a big step forward.

RAD DAD JOKES

What's the difference between a man's wallet before and after kids? There are pictures where the money used to be.

What did the baby corn say to the mama corn? Where's popcorn?

I wish my gray hair started in Las Vegas because what happens in Vegas, stays in Vegas.

What vegetable is cool, but not that cool? Radish.

My kid is blaming me for ruining their birthday. That's ridiculous, I didn't even know it was today!

I haven't spoken to my wife in four years. I thought it would be rude to interrupt her!

My kid gave me a World's Best Dad mug. At least she inherited my sense of humor.

When a toddler reaches the "why?" stage, it's like opening a bottle of champagne—once it's uncorked, there's no going back.

What do you call two monkeys who share an Amazon Prime account? Prime mates.

You can't spell parentry without "try."

How do you measure the mass of an influencer's following? By Instagrams!

How do you teach kids about taxes? Eat 38% of their ice cream.

Two sheep walk into a baaaa.

What do you call a beehive without an exit? Un-bee-lievable.

What did the seal with one fin say to the shark? If seal is broken, do not consume.

RAD DAD JOKES

I wish my kids weren't offended by my Frozen jokes. They really need to let it go!

Why did the football coach go to the bank? To get his quarter back.

Why can't a leopard hide? He's always spotted.

Air used to be free at the gas station, now it costs $2.50. You want to know why? Inflation.

I tried to get a smart car the other day but they sold out too fast. Why? I guess I'm just a bit slow.

I told my wife that a husband is like a fine wine and we get better with age. The next day she locked me in the cellar.

RAD DAD JOKES

Why does a husband lead a dog's life? He comes in with muddy feet, gets comfortable by the fire, and waits to be fed.

Did you hear about the claustrophobic astronaut? He just wanted a bit more space.

What does the stork do once he's delivered the baby? He lies on the couch and drinks a beer!

How many telemarketers does it take to change a light bulb? Only one, but he has to do it during dinner.

Why did the orange lose the race? It ran out of juice.

Why are fish so smart? They live in schools!

What's the best thing about Switzerland? I don't know, but the flag is a big plus.

RAD DAD JOKES

Why did the man fall down the well? Because he couldn't see that well!

Why do peppers make such good archers? Because they habanero.

What did the sink tell the toilet? You look flushed!

Where do boats go when they're sick? To the dock.

What has ears but cannot hear? A cornfield!

Why was 6 afraid of 7? Because 7 ate 9!

I'm so good at sleeping that I do it with my eyes closed.

Try the seafood diet—you see food, then you eat it.

What do you call a pencil with two erasers? Pointless.

Did you hear the one about the roof? Never mind, it's over your head.

I hated facial hair but then it grew on me.

It really takes guts to be an organ donor.

Did you hear the rumor about butter? Well, I'm not going to go spreading it!

What did the plumber say to the singer? Nice pipes.

How do you deal with a fear of speed bumps? You slowly get over it.

I ordered a chicken and an egg online. I'll let you know.

I'm reading an anti-gravity book. I can't put it down!

I would avoid the sushi if I were you. It's a little fishy!

What's Forrest Gump's password? 1forrest1.

What do houses wear? An address.

What did the two pieces of bread say on their wedding day? It was loaf at first sight.

What kind of shoes does a lazy person wear? Loafers.

What did the ocean say to the beach? Nothing, it just waved.

What happens when a snowman throws a tantrum? He has a meltdown.

RAD DAD JOKES

Why did the fisherman order the halibut? Just for the halibut!

Why is Peter Pan always flying? Because he Neverlands.

What do you call a sleeping bull? A bulldozer.

How do you throw a party in outer space? You planet.

Why was the broom late to class? It over-swept.

How do you make an octopus laugh? With ten-tickles!

What do you say to a rabbit on its birthday? Hoppy Birthday!

What type of tree fits in your hand? A palm tree.

Why couldn't the bicycle stand up by itself? It was two tired!

Want to hear a joke about construction? I'm still working on it!

What do you call a fake noodle? An impasta.

How does a lawyer say goodbye? I'll be suing ya!

You can't trust atoms. They make up everything!

Can I dive in this pool? It deep-ends.

What did the buffalo say to its son when he left? Bison!

Why do vampires always seem sick? They're coffin.

What musical instrument do you find in the bathroom? A tuba toothpaste!

Which state has the most streets? Rhode Island.

Why do bees have sticky hair? Because they use a honeycomb.

Why do melons have weddings? They cantaloupe!

What did the police officer say to her belly button? You're under a vest!

What do you call a fibbing cat? A lion.

If a child refuses to nap, are they guilty of resisting a rest?

How do you make seven even? You take away the s.

Did you hear about the outlet who got in a fight with the power cord? He thought he could socket to him.

What kind of cars do eggs drive? Yolkswagens.

Where do math teachers go on vacation? Times Square.

Why was the stadium so hot after the game? Because all the fans left.

The coach went to the bank to get his quarterback.

The first thing Santa's elves learn in school is their elf-abet.

Ghosts are bad liars because you can see right through them.

Shouldn't the "roof" of your mouth actually be called the ceiling?

All vampires keep their money in a special place—the blood bank.

The pony couldn't sing because it was a little horse.

If two vegetarians get in an argument, is it still called beef?

RAD DAD JOKES

RIP boiling water, you will be mist.

I told my doctor I heard buzzing, but she said it's just a bug that's going around.

I ate a clock the other day. It was very time consuming.

I have a clean conscious—it's never been used.

I once wrote a song about a tortilla, but it's more of a wrap.

You can tell it's a dogwood tree from its bark.

I don't curse. I speak fluent trucker with a sailor dialect and a construction accent.

They say that 3/2 people are bad at fractions.

I'm worried for the calendar because its days are numbered.

Dear Math, it's time to grow up and solve your own problems.

I only know 25 letters of the alphabet—I don't know y.

I used to play piano by ear, but now I use my hands.

Why were the utensils stuck together? They were spooning.

How do celebrities stay cool? They have many fans.

Why did the picture go to prison? Because it was framed.

RAD DAD JOKES

How does a hurricane see? With one eye.

Where do polar bears keep their money? The snow bank.

What's a tornado's favorite game? Twister!

What do you call a funny mountain? Hill-arious.

What gets wetter the more it dries? A towel.

What rock group has four men who don't sing? Mount Rushmore.

My boss told me to have a good day, so I went home!

What do you call cheese that isn't yours? Nacho cheese.

Did you get your haircut? No, I got them all cut.

I was wondering why the frisbee kept getting bigger and bigger. Then it hit me.

Why do Dads feel the need to tell such bad jokes? They just want to help you become a groan up.

What do you call a dad who studied dad jokes? A sigh-entist.

How many apples grow on a tree? All of them!

I talk to myself because sometimes I just need expert advice.

I used to be addicted to the hokey-pokey until I turned myself around.

RAD DAD JOKES

What concert would cost only 45 cents? 50 Cent featuring Nickelback!

What do you call someone who tells dad jokes but isn't a dad? A faux pa.

I could tell a joke about pizza, but it's a little cheesy.

If you see a crime at an Apple store, are you an iWitness?

Spring is here! I got so excited that I wet my plants.

I had to sell my vacuum cleaner. All it was doing was gathering dust.

Do you know how many people are dead at a cemetery? All of them.

RAD DAD JOKES

Me: I'll call you later.
Dad: Don't call me later, call me Dad.

If the early bird gets the worm, I'll sleep in until there's pancakes.

The wedding was so beautiful, even the cake was in tiers.

Why are spiders so smart? They can find everything on the web.

What do you call a toothless bear? A gummy bear!

What do you give a sick lemon? Lemon-aid.

What did the nose tell the finger? Stop picking on me!

RAD DAD JOKES

Why can't your hand be 12 inches long? Because then it would be a foot.

What kind of car does a sheep like to drive? A Lamborghini.

What key is used to open bananas? A monkey.

What has four wheels and flies? A garbage truck.

How do you talk to a giant? You use big words!

What kind of milk comes from a pampered cow? Spoiled milk.

What's a sea monster's favorite lunch? Fish and ships.

What do you call an alligator in a vest? An investigator.

Can a kangaroo jump higher than a house? Of course, houses can't jump.

Why are pigs so bad at sports? They always hog the ball.

Why shouldn't you tell an egg a joke? It'll crack up.

What's a foot long and slippery? A slipper.

Why did the scarecrow win an award? He was outstanding in his field.

What's orange and sounds like a parrot? A carrot!

How does a penguin build a house? Igloos it together.

Why is no one friends with Dracula? He's a pain in the neck.

Where do you learn all about ice cream?
Sundae school.

What does a baby computer call his father?
Data.

After an unsuccessful harvest, why did the farmer decide to try a career in music?
Because he had a ton of sick beets.

I only seem to get sick on weekdays. I must have a weekend immune system.

My friend was showing me his tool shed and pointed to a ladder. "That's my stepladder," he said. "I never knew my real ladder."

What do you call a Frenchman wearing sandals? Philippe Flop.

Why is it so cheap to throw a party at a haunted house? Because the ghosts bring all the boos.

RAD DAD JOKES

What brand of underwear do scientists wear? Kelvin Klein.

Which days are the strongest? Saturday and Sunday. The rest are weekdays.

I just found out I'm colorblind. The news came out of the purple!

Did you know your pupils are the last part to stop working when you die? They dilate.

My wife asked me the other day where I got so much candy. I said, "I always have a few Twix up my sleeve."

How do cows stay up to date? They read the Moo-spaper.

What's the difference between a well-dressed man on a unicycle and a poorly dressed man on a bicycle? Attire.

I hate my job—all I do is crush cans all day. It's soda pressing.

Where do pirates get their hooks? Secondhand stores.

Of all the inventions of the last 100 years, the dry erase board has to be the most remarkable.

Who were the greenest Presidents in US history? The Bushes.

My hotel tried to charge me ten dollars extra for air conditioning. That wasn't cool.

I found a wooden shoe in my toilet today. It was clogged.

If I ever find the doctor who screwed up my limb replacement surgery…I'll kill him with my bear hands.

Did you know that the first French fries weren't cooked in France? They were cooked in Greece.

This morning, Siri said, "Don't call me, Shirley." I accidentally left my phone in Airplane mode.

It's easy to convince ladies not to eat Tide Pods, but harder to deter gents.

I asked my date to meet me at the gym but she never showed up. I guess the two of us aren't going to work out.

The difference between a numerator and a denominator is a short line. Only a fraction of people will understand this.

I just broke up with my mathematician girlfriend. She was obsessed with an X.

I can't take my dog to the pond anymore because the ducks keep attacking him. That's what I get for buying a pure bread dog.

To whoever stole my copy of Microsoft Office, I will find you. You have my Word.

I used to run a dating service for chickens. But I was struggling to make hens meet.

If prisoners could take their own mug shots…They'd be called cellfies.

Have you heard about those new corduroy pillows? They're making headlines.

If a pig loses its voice, does it become disgruntled?

A panic-stricken man explained to his doctor, "You have to help me, I think I'm shrinking." "Now settle down," the doctor calmly told him. "You'll just have to learn to be a little patient."

What do you call a bundle of hay in a church? Christian Bale.

A ship carrying red paint and a ship carrying blue paint collide in the middle of the ocean. Both crews were marooned.

What's a guitar player's favorite Italian food? Strum-boli.

How does cereal pay its bills? With Chex.

Have you heard about the restaurant on the moon? Great food, no atmosphere.

People in Athens rarely get up before sunrise. Dawn is tough on Greece.

Why did the alternate universe Spider-Man do so well on his driving test? He's an excellent parallel Parker.

Never date a tennis player. Love means nothing to them.

What's a lawyer's favorite drink? Subpoena colada.

What did Yoda say when he saw himself in 4K? HDMI.

What do you call a wizard who's really bad at football? Fumbledore.

What's blue and not very heavy? Light blue.

I don't get why bakers aren't wealthier. They make so much dough.

How do flat-earthers travel? On a plane.

If you're feeling depressed, try drinking a gallon of water before you go to sleep. It'll give you a reason to get out of bed in the morning.

My wife left me because of my obsession with pasta. I'm feeling cannelloni right now.

Imagine if you walked into a bar and there was a long line of people waiting to take a swing at you. That's the punch line.

I was playing chess with my friend and he said, "Let's make this interesting." We stopped playing chess.

Why didn't the vampire attack Taylor Swift? She had bad blood.

I'm attaching a light to the ceiling, but I'm afraid I'll probably screw it up.

I hate it when people say age is only a number. Age is clearly a word.

Someone complimented my parking today! They left a sweet note on my windshield that said, "Parking Fine."

I was excited to hear Apple might start selling its own cars until I learned they wouldn't support Windows.

I just applied for a job down at the diner. I told them I really bring a lot to the table.

An apple a day keeps the doctor away. At least it does if you throw it hard enough.

Cop: I'm arresting you for downloading the entire Wikipedia. Me: Wait! I can explain everything!

What has five toes and isn't your foot? My foot.

Not to brag bustays t I made six figures last year. I was also named worst employee at the toy factory.

Ever since we started quarantining, I have only been telling inside jokes.

My landlord told me we need to talk about the heating bill. "Sure," I said. "My door is always open."

I built a model of Mount Everest and my son asked if it was to scale. "No," I said. "It's to look at."

My friend claims he glued himself to his autobiography. I don't believe him, but that's his story and he's sticking to it.

When I was a kid, my mother told me I could be anyone I wanted to be. Turns out, identity theft is a crime.

A century ago, two brothers decided it was possible to fly. And as you can see, they were Wright.

Why did the Invisible Man turn down a job offer? He couldn't see himself doing it.

I'm reading a horror story in braille. Something bad is going to happen, I can just feel it.

Is anyone looking to buy a Delorean? Good shape, good mileage. Only driven from time to time.

During my calculus test, I had to sit between identical twins. It was hard to differentiate between them.

Does anybody know where a guy can find a person to hang out with, talk to, and enjoy spending time with? I'm just asking for a friend.

When I die, I want to be cremated. It's my last chance to have a smoking hot body.

"Just say NO to drugs!" Well, if I'm talking to drugs, I probably already said yes.

I once saw a one-handed man in a second-hand store. I told him, "I don't think they have what you're looking for, sir."

What do you call a sad cup of coffee? Depresso.

What did one monocle say to the other monocle? Let's get together and make a spectacle of ourselves.

What kind of fruit do ghosts like? Boo-berries.

How come the Hulk doesn't lose his pants when he transforms? The experiment altered his jeans.

I just spent $300 on a limo and learned it doesn't come with a driver. I can't believe I have nothing to chauffer it.

A buddy asked how many fish I caught. I told him it's not polite to fish and tell.

Just got back from a job interview where I was asked if I could perform under pressure. I said I wasn't too sure about that but I could do a wicked "Bohemian Rhapsody."

At the job interview, they asked me, "Where do you see yourself in five years?" I told him, "I think we'll still be using mirrors in five years."

How many clickbait articles does it take to change a lightbulb? The answer will shock you!

How do you make a waterbed bouncier? Add spring water.

I always knock on the fridge door before opening it just in case there's a salad dressing.

Where do dads store their dad jokes? In the dad-a-base.

I tried to start a professional hide and seek team, but it didn't work out. Turns out, good players are hard to find.

Women should not have children after 36—really, 36 children are enough.

What happens when frogs park illegally? They get toad.

Lance isn't that common a name these days, but in medieval times, they were called lance-a-lot.

I had an appointment to see my psychic next week, but she just called to cancel. She said I won't be able to make it.

I used to be addicted to soap, but I'm clean now.

I wanted my kids to watch the orchestra, but I had to turn it off—too much sax and violins.

A cop started crying while he was writing me a ticket. I asked him why and he said, "It's a moving violation."

Swords will never go obsolete. They're cutting-edge technology.

I asked the IT guy, "How do you make a Motherboard?" He said, "I tell her about my job."

My grief counselor died the other day. He was so good at his job, I don't even care.

Give a man a plane ticket and he flies for the day. Push him out of the plane at 3,000 feet and he'll fly for the rest of his life.

Why should you never brush your teeth with your left hand? Because a toothbrush works better.

As I get older, I remember all the people I lost along the way. Maybe a career as a tour guide was not the right choice.

What do you call it when James Bond takes a bath? Bubble 07.

30% of pet owners let their pets sleep in their bed. I tried it and my goldfish died.

What's the difference between a literalist and a kleptomaniac? A literalist takes everything literally. A kleptomaniac takes everything literally.

I just found out Albert Einstein existed. My whole life I thought he was a theoretical physicist.

I went to a smoke shop only to discover it'd been replaced by an apparel store. Clothes, but no cigar.

I was reading a terrific book about an immortal dog the other day. It was impossible to put down.

What do you call someone who refuses to fart in public? A private tutor.

They say that breakfast is the most important meal of the day. Well, not if it's poisoned. Then the antidote becomes the most important.

The guy who stole my diary just died. My thoughts are with his family.

Do you know the last thing my grandfather said to me before he kicked the bucket? "Grandson, watch how far I can kick this bucket."

If you donate a kidney, everybody loves you and you're a total hero. But try donating five kidneys and suddenly everyone is yelling and the police get called.

I have a fish that can breakdance. Only for ten seconds though, and only once.

My friend said that if he went off a cliff, it would be on his own accord. It's a good thing he drives a Civic.

In my free time, I like to help blind people. Verb, not adjective.

I like to spend my weekends playing chess with elderly men in the park. But it's becoming more difficult. You try finding exactly 32 old guys.

What do you call bears with no ears? B.

What's the difference between a wizard who raises the undead and a sexy vampire? One is a necromancer and the other is a neck romancer.

A man walks into a magic forest and tries to cut down a talking tree. "You can't cut me down," the tree complains. "I'm a talking tree!" The man responds, "You may be a talking tree, but you will dialogue."

I heard Sony's coming out with a new console during the pandemic. It's called the Plaguestation 5.

When my Uncle Frank died, he wanted his remains to be buried in his favorite beer mug. His last wish was to be Frank in Stein.

A man walks into a bar. The bartender asks, "What do you want?" The man says, "Oh, just some fruit punch." The bartender sighs and shakes his head, "If you want punch, you're gonna have to wait in line." The man looks around, but there is no punch line.

I just got my doctor's test results and I'm really upset. Turns out, I'm not going to be a doctor.

I think my wife is putting glue on my antique guns collection. She denies it but I'm sticking to my guns.

My wife left a note on the fridge that said, "This isn't working." I'm not sure what she's talking about. I opened the fridge door and it's working fine!

My wife told me she didn't understand cloning. I told her, "That makes two of us."

My wife told me she'll slam my head on the keyboard if I don't get off the computer. I'm not too worried, I think she's jokinlkjhfakljniyoao78yv87dfaoyuofaytdf.

My wife gave birth three times and still fits in her prom dress from high school. I gave birth zero times and I don't fit in my pants from March.

When I see the names of lovers engraved on a tree, I don't find it cute or romantic. I find it weird how many people take knives with them on dates.

After dinner, my wife asked if I could clear the table. I needed a running start, but I made it.

Why didn't the astronaut come home to his wife? He needed his space.

My wife gave me an ultimatum: Her or my addiction to sweets. The decision was a piece of cake.

My wife told me to quit doing my terrible Arnold impression, but don't worry, I'll be back.

"Just look at that couple down the road," a wife told her husband. "He keeps holding her hand, kissing her, holding the door for her. Why can't you do that?" "Are you insane?" he responded. "I barely know the woman!"

I was sitting on the back porch with my wife when I suddenly blurted out, "I love you." "Is that you or the beer talking?" she asked. I answered, "It's me… talking to my beer."

"Siri," I asked my phone, "why am I so bad with women?" She responded, "I'm Bixby, you moron."

My wife and I were out to dinner and the waitress started flirting with me. "She obviously has COVID," my wife said. "Why?" I asked. "Because she has no taste."

Marriage involves three rings: The engagement ring, the wedding ring, and the suffer-ring.

"Your wife and daughter look like twins," my friend said. "Well," I replied, "they were separated at birth.

One friend complained to another, "All my husband and I do anymore is fight. I have been so upset that I have lost 20 pounds." "If it's that bad, why don't you just leave him?" asked the second friend. "I'd like to lose another fifteen pounds first."

I bought Spotify premium for an uninterrupted music experience. But I still hear my wife's bickering between songs.

I can always tell when my wife is lying just by looking at her. I can also tell when she's standing.

My wife told me that I twist everything she says to my advantage. I take that as a compliment.

My ex and I had a very amicable divorce. I know this because when I posted on Facebook, "I'm getting a divorce," she was the first one to like it.

My wife and I have decided not to have kids. The kids are taking it pretty badly.

My daughter just shrieked at me, "Daaaaaad, you haven't listened to a word I have said, have you?" What an odd way to begin a conversation.

RAD DAD JOKES

I have a great joke about nepotism. But I'll only tell it to my kids.

Son: Dad, can you explain to me what a solar eclipse is?
Me: No sun.

What happened when the ten-year-old cannibal spilled his soup? His mother gave him an earful.

I would like to have kids one day. I don't think I could stand them any longer than that, though.

I wonder what my parents did to fight boredom before the internet. I asked my eighteen brothers and sisters but they didn't have any idea either.

My parents raised me as an only child. Which really annoyed my younger brother.

A kid decided to burn his house down. His dad watched, tears in his eyes. He put his arm around the mom and said, "That's arson."

My dad died because he couldn't remember his blood type. He kept insisting we "be positive," but it's just so hard without him.

Today I decided to visit my childhood home. I asked the residents if I could come inside because I was feeling nostalgic, but they refused and slammed the door on my face. My parents are the worst.

I tried to explain to my 4-year-old son that it's perfectly normal to accidentally poop your pants. But he's still making fun of me.

"What's your name, son?" The principal asked his student. The kid replied, "D-D-D-Dav-Dav-David, sir." "Do you have a stutter?" the principal asked. The student answered, "No sir, my dad has a stutter but the guy who registered my name was a real jerk."

RAD DAD JOKES

Yesterday, I was washing the car with my son. He said, "Dad, can't you just use a sponge?"

I wasn't close to my father when he died. Which is lucky because he stepped on a landmine.

Singing in the shower is fun until you get soap in your mouth. Then it's a soap opera.

What do you call a fish wearing a bowtie? Sofishticated.

Concerned that his son was spending too much time on video games, John's dad told him, "When Abe Lincoln was your age, he was studying books by the light of the fireplace." "Oh yeah?" the son retorts. "Well, when Abe Lincoln was your age, he was President of the United States."

A father tells his son that he was adopted. "I want to meet my biological parents," the son demands. "We are your biological parents," the father responds. "Now pack up, the new ones will pick you up in twenty minutes."

A son tells his father, "I have an imaginary girlfriend." The father sighs and says, "You know, you could do better." "Thanks Dad," the son says. "That means a lot." The father shakes his head and goes, "I was talking to your girlfriend."

What has more letters than the alphabet? The post office.

I thought the dryer was shrinking my clothes. Turns out it was the refrigerator all along.

What do you call a factory that makes okay products? A satisfactory.

What did the janitor say when he jumped out of the closet? Supplies!

Have you heard about the chocolate record player? It sounds pretty sweet.

What did one wall say to the other? I'll meet you at the corner.

What did the zero say to the eight? That belt looks good on you.

Where do fruits go on vacation? Pear-is!

How do you get a squirrel to like you? Act like a nut.

What does a sprinter eat before a race? Nothing, they fast!

What do you call a poor Santa Claus? St. Nickel-less.

I got carded at a liquor store, and my Blockbuster card accidentally fell out. The cashier said never mind.

My wife is really mad at the fact that I have no sense of direction. So, I packed up my stuff and right!

Why don't eggs tell jokes? They'd crack each other up.

What do you call someone with no body and no nose? Nobody knows.

What did one hat say to the other? Stay here! I'm going on ahead.

Why did Billy get fired from the banana factory? He kept throwing away the bent ones.

What does a lemon say when it answers the phone? Yellow!

This graveyard looks overcrowded. People must be dying to get in.

Kid: Dad, can you put the cat out?
Dad: I didn't know it was on fire.

How does a taco say grace? Lettuce pray.

What time did the man go to the dentist? Tooth hurt-y.

Why did the math book look so sad? Because of all of its problems!

What kind of shoes do ninjas wear? Sneakers.

Do you think swimming with sharks is expensive? Swimming with sharks cost me an arm and a leg.

Do you want a box for your leftovers? No, but I'll wrestle you for them.

That car looks nice but the muffler seems exhausted.

Shout out to my fingers. I can count on all of them.

What country's capital is growing the fastest? Ireland. Every day it's Dublin.

Did you hear about the kidnapping at school? It's okay, he woke up.

A cheeseburger walks into a bar. The bartender says, "Sorry, we don't serve food here."

I once got fired from a canned juice company. Apparently, I couldn't concentrate.

I'm reading a book about anti-gravity. It's impossible to put down!

What's a robot's favorite snack? Computer chips.

Did you hear about the guy who invented the knock-knock joke? He won the no-bell prize.

I had a neck brace fitted years ago and I have never looked back since.

You know, people say they pick their nose, but I feel like I was just born with mine.

Why can't you hear a psychiatrist using the bathroom? Because the 'P' is silent.

What's the best smelling insect? A deodor-ant.

I used to be a personal trainer. Then I gave my too weak notice.

Did I tell you the time I fell in love during a backflip? I was heels over head!

I was going to tell a time-traveling joke, but you all didn't like it.

What do you call a belt made of watches? A waist of time.

What happens when a strawberry gets run over crossing the street? Traffic jam.

Whenever I try to eat healthy, a chocolate bar looks at me and Snickers.

What does garlic do when it gets hot? It takes its cloves off.

How much does it cost Santa to park his sleigh? Nothing, it's on the house.

Mountains aren't just funny. They're hill areas.

Why are piggy banks so wise? They're filled with common cents.

How do you get a decent price on a sled? You have toboggan.

What do you call a hot dog on wheels? Fast food!

Where do young trees go to learn? Elementree school.

Did you hear about the circus fire? It was in tents.

What's the best way to watch a flyfishing tournament? Live stream.

What's an astronaut's favorite part of a computer? The space bar.

I don't play soccer because I enjoy the sport. I'm just doing it for kicks!

Why are elevator jokes so classic and good? They work on many levels.

What did the coffee report to the police? A mugging.

What did the fish say when he hit the wall? Dam.

I tried to make up a joke about a ghost but I couldn't. It had plenty of spirit but no body.

Two windmills were sitting on a hill the one asks the one humming do you have a favorite song? The one says well, all my life I have been a heavy metal fan.

Today at the bank, an older lady asked me to check her balance so, I pushed her over.

I was walking down the beach when I heard a swimmer yelling for help with a shark circling him. I just laughed...I knew that shark wasn't going to help him.

How many storm troopers does it take to change a lightbulb? None. Because they are all on the dark side.

Dad: What's the difference between a piano, a tuna, and a pot of glue?
Me: Idk
Dad: You can tuna piano but you can't piano a tuna.
Me: What about the pot of glue?
Dad: I knew you'd get stuck on that.

Are you from Tennessee because you're the only ten I see.

Did you hear about the guy who went to the doctor for a headache? The doctor examined his ear and found money. The doctor kept pulling and pulling it out until he had $1,999. Then the doctor says no wonder you're not feeling two grand!

Why did the egg have a day off? Because it was Fryday.

What do you call the security guards for Samsung? Guardians of the galaxy.

What do you call a ghost who works? I can't tell you because he can't see himself doing it!

What do you call a really fat psychic? A four-chin teller.

My friend is the best at Russian roulette. He only lost once.

What do you call a rabbit with fleas? Bugs Bunny.

There were three friends and one stutters, the other one owns a motorcycle and the third one's name is Harambe. One day the one with the motorcycle asks "Hey, you guys want to go on a ride?" and they both said yes. The one that stutters is in the middle and Harambe is in the back. When they go the guy driving says "Hold on" as he pulls a wheely and ask's if they are having fun and he hears HA HA HA! He decides to pull another wheely and he hears HA HA HA! again so he pulls a wheely a third time and he hears, "HA HA HARAMBE fell off two miles back!"

You are on a horse riding full gallop. Next to you is a giraffe at full gallop. Behind you is a lion on your tail. What do you do? Get off the carousel.

I used to date a girl with one leg who worked at a brewery. She was in charge of the hops.

What's the cutest creature in the sea? A cuddlefish.

A dad told his son that they were having Himalayan deer steak for dinner. The son said, "Where did you find a Himalayan deer?" Dad responds, "I found Himalayan on the road."

I had a horse named Mayo and Mayo neighed.

The owner of the tuxedo store kept hovering over me when I was browsing so I asked him to leave me alone. He said "Fine, suit yourself!"

I bought a dog but it barked so I had to give him to the trees.

Have you heard about the Italian chef who died? He pasta away.

Why did the coffee taste like dirt? Because it was GROUND just a couple minutes ago. Where has this joke "BEAN" all my life!

Teacher: What family does the Zebra belong to?
Student: Can't say, none of the families in our neighborhood owns a Zebra.

What word can you make shorter by adding two letters? Short.

Did you know diarrhea is hereditary? It runs in your genes.

If your house is cold, why not just stand in the corner? It's 90 degrees there!

What do call a criminal landing an airplane? Condescending.

If you're an American in the kitchen then what are you in the bathroom? European.

My ex-wife still misses me but her aims getting better.

What do grapes sing at Christmas? "Tis the season to be jelly fa-la-la-la-la-la-la-la."

What did the grape say when it got stepped on? Nothing, it let out just a little whine.

Did you hear about the fragile myth? It was busted.

What do you call an elephant in a telephone booth? Stuck.

Did you hear about the famous pickle? He's a really big dill!

A drug dealer gave me laces. I don't know what he did to them but I have been tripping all day.

How do you help a crocodile if it gets hurt? Give it Gatorade.

RAD DAD JOKES

What did the picture say to the wall? First, they frame me then they hang me.

What did the traffic light say to the other? Stop looking, I'm changing!

What did Elvis say to his landscaper? Thank you for the mulch!

Why didn't the lifeguard save the hippie? He was too far out!

Why couldn't the tree get on his computer? Because he could not LOG ON.

What's the skeletons favorite road? A dead end!

A man walked into a bar with a parrot on his shoulder. The bartender said, "Does the animal talk?" The parrot said, "I don't know."

RAD DAD JOKES

Why don't skeletons go trick or treating?
Because they have no body to go with.

Me: I want to write when I grow up.
Dad: Why don't you left instead?

How many ears does Captain Kirk have?
Three. The left ear, the right ear, and the final frontier.

What did the mother broom say to the baby broom? It's time to go to sweep.

I kept wondering why the ball was floating in the air towards me. Then, it hit me.

Why did the computer go to the doctor?
Because he had a virus.

How can you tell where a man's former wife died? Ex marks the spot!

RAD DAD JOKES

What do you get when you cross a spider and an ocean? A trench-ila.

Today, my son asked, "Can I have a bookmark?" and I burst into tears. 11 years old and he still doesn't know my name is Brian.

Why can't the Mexican shoot an arrow? Because he doesn't habanero.

Why did the baseball player get fired? He ran three bases than walked home.

Hey is your refrigerator running?!?! You better go catch it.

Did you hear about the movie constipation. No? It hasn't come out yet.

What do you need to make a highway in an art studio? A mile marker.

How do you make holy water? You boil the hell out of it.

Why was Mac OS so worried? Because he couldn't Finder.

A dyslexic man walks into a bra

What letter in the alphabet has the most water. C.

How do you make Anti-freeze? Hide her nightgown.

My dog used to chase people on the bike a lot. Finally, I had enough and took his bike away.

What did the scared person say on the long hike? We're not out of the woods yet.

So don't go blaming anyone for the road you travel. It's your own asphalt!

Why do some couples go to the gym? Because some relationships don't work out.

How did the tornado fail the test? He blew it!

I tried to bring zombies into my house. But the problem was, they couldn't get in because of the living room!

Why couldn't the safe laugh? Because it wouldn't budge.

What's the best snack for recess. For me, it's a recess pieces.

I tried to make a tire joke but I was too tired.

What do you get when you cross an elephant and a rhino? Elephino!

What did the body do before going on vacation. It got organ-ised.

How did the burger get pregnant. It didn't use condiments.

How much does a chimney cost. Nothing it's on the house.

Did you see Michael Phelps twist his ankle? He was Olympian.

Why don't fish play basketball? Because they are scared of the net.

What begins with an E and only contains one letter? Envelope.

What do you call someone with no body and no nose? Nobody knows.

My teacher told me to turn in my essay. I told her I ain't no snitch.

Me: Dad, will you make me a sandwich?
Dad: POOF…you're a sandwich.

What did the teacher say to the grape? Give me a raisin.

Hey, can you tie your shoes. I don't want you falling for anyone else but me.

Why did the toilet paper get stuck in the road? Because it was in a crack.

What vehicle does the devil drive? A HELLicopter.

I would tell u a joke about a bell, but it's just ringing in my ear saying not to.

Why did the boy bear have a crush on the girl bear? She was beary pretty!

Why do scuba divers fall backwards out of the boat? Because if they fall frontwards, they'd still be in the boat.

Why can't you fight a bear. Because its unbearable.

Kid: What's it like having the world's most amazing son?
Dad: I don't know. Why don't you ask grandpa.
Kid: Yeah, Uncle John is pretty cool.
Dad: You're grounded.

What do you call an American bee. A USB.

What do you say to a handicap kid wearing camo? You can hide but you can't run!

Why was the lipoma temped? He just couldn't re-cyst!

Two cannibals were eating a clown. One says to the other, "Does this taste funny?"

What do you call it when a buff man loses his wife? Tough times.

What cartoon on Cartoon Network curses the most? Roadrunner! Beep Beep!

RAD DAD JOKES

A nuke went to a party once! He had a blast!

What do you call a man with a rubber toe? Roberto.

What do you call it when you cannot go pee? Urine trouble.

Why does a milking stool only have three legs? Because the cow has the utter one.

What type of bagel can fly? A plane bagel.

Want to hear a plant joke? Oh sorry, I have to leaf but I wood have liked to tell you.

How do you know if you have a sneaky pepper? He's jalapeño your business.

What's the cheapest slab of meat? Deer balls, because it's under a buck.

Remember kids, when you see an orphan punch them in the face. What are they going to do? Tell their parents?

How do you unlock a bathroom when it's locked? You use a dookey.

Why was the house cleaner wearing seashells? B-shells were too small.

What do you call a Mexican who lost his car? Carlos.

What do you call a naughty lamb dressed up like a skeleton for Halloween? Baaad to the bone.

What do you call it when a group of apes starts a company? Monkey business.

My wife asked me to stop singing "Wonderwall" to her. I said maybe.

RAD DAD JOKES

Knock knock.
Who's there?
Joe.
Joe who?
Joe mama.

Did you hear about the man who was attacked by a bear? He bearly survived.

Is your face from McDonald's? Cause I'm loving it!

Want to hear a cat joke. Just kitten.

Why did the teddy bear turn down a slice of cake? He was stuffed.

What do you call a witch on the beach? Sandwich.

Cantaloupe tonight, Dad's got the car!

What kind if cheese do you use to disguise a small horse? Mascarpone.

What's an astronaut's favorite board game? Moonopoly.

How did Jesus make tea? Hebrewed it.

Which bear is the most condescending? A Pan-duh!

What kind of noise does a witch's vehicle make? Brrrroooom, brrroooom.

Two guys walked into a bar. The third guy ducked.

How do you get a country girl's attention? A tractor.

What do you call a pudgy psychic? A four-chin teller.

RAD DAD JOKES

What kind of drink can be bitter and sweet? Reali-tea.

What would the Terminator be called in his retirement? The Exterminator.

What do you call an angry musician flipping someone off? A songbird.

Why was the color green notoriously single? It was always so jaded.

Sundays are always a little sad, but the day before is a sadder day.

5/4 of people admit they're bad at fractions.

Why did the bedding hide their relationship? They just wanted something pillow-key!

I have been thinking about taking up meditation. I figure it's better than sitting around doing nothing.

RAD DAD JOKES

Dogs can't operate MRI machines, but catscan.

What did the flowers do when the bride walked down the aisle? They rose.

What does Rockin' Robin do when she's bored? Tweet.

How do you row a canoe filled with puppies? Bring out the doggy paddle.

What has one head, one foot, and four legs? A bed.

Sore throats are a pain in the neck.

Knock knock.
Who's there?
Ayatollah.
Ayatollah who?
Ayatollah you already.

RAD DAD JOKES

What's a crafty dancer's favorite hobby? Cutting a rug.

What kind of music do chiropractors like? Hip-pop.

Why is cold water so insecure? Because it's never called hot.

What did the accountant say while auditing a document? This is taxing.

I signed up for a marathon, but how will I know if it's the real deal or just a run through?

What did the drummer call his twin daughters? Anna One, Anna Two!

What did the juicer say to the orange during self-quarantine? Can't wait to squeeze you!

Someone told me that I should write a book. I said, "That's a novel concept."

I know a lot of jokes about retired people, but none of them work.

Why are spiders so smart? They can find everything on the web.

What do you call two octopuses that look the same? Itenticle.

My son asked me to put his shoes on, but I don't think they'll fit me.

I have been bored recently, so I decided to take up fencing. The neighbors keep demanding that I put it back.

What do you call an unpredictable camera? A loose Canon.

What do sprinters eat before a race? Nothing, they fast.

What did one Dorito farmer say to the other? "Cool Ranch!"

People are usually shocked that I have a Police record. But I love their greatest hits!

I told my girlfriend she drew on her eyebrows too high. She seemed surprised.

What do you call a fibbing cat? A lion.

Why shouldn't you write with a broken pencil? Because it's pointless.

What's the most patriotic sport? Flag football.

Why did the envelope take so long to get ready? It had to get addressed.

RAD DAD JOKES

What does a karate master get rewarded with while driving? A seat belt.

What did the husband say to his wife right after getting LASIK surgery? "Aren't you a sight for sore eyes?"

What do lions use to look at their manes? Mirroars.

What did the dad say when his golden retriever was caught eating a hot dog? "It's a dog-eat-dog world out there."

Do mascara and lipstick ever argue? Sure, but then they makeup.

What piece on the playground is always exhausted? The tire swing.

Why did two tall people get along so well? They could really see eye to eye.

Why was the gossip disliked at the coffee shop? She always spilled the tea.

What does a writer have in common with a football player? Anxiety over a rough draft.

Where do wasps like to get lunch? A bee-stro.

Why would doors do well on social media? Everyone looks for their handles.

Which bathroom appliance would be the worst life preserver? The sink.

Why was the dad sitting on a pack of playing cards? His kid asked him to sit on the deck.

What kind of bird is always getting hurt? The owl.

What's either a really gross animal issue OR an impressive, magical school? Hogwarts.

What did the dishwasher say to the oven after a productive day? "You've been on fire!"

Why did the cashier rip money in half? They were asked to break a bill.

What did one furniture maker say to another during a tense discussion? "Let's table this."

Why was the ghost so tired? He worked the graveyard shift.

Why do pancakes always win at baseball? They have the best batter.

Why couldn't the couple get married at the library? It was all booked up.

How did the dad prank his daughter using fake dog poop on April Fool's Day? He told her to look out for her new sham-poo in the shower.

What did the air conditioner say when it met a celebrity? I'm a big fan.

What was Sherlock Holmes' favorite protein source? Mystery meat.

What did the dryer say to the boring duvet cover that just got out of the washer? "Don't be such a wet blanket."

Why was the cow such a heartthrob on the farm? He was a s-moo-th talker.

What's a writer's favorite train station? Penn Station.

What was said about the messy, angry man who was eating a can of Pringles? He's got a chip on his shoulder.

What's it called when kittens get stuck in a tree? A cat-astrophe.

Why is sand so optimistic? It has a can-dune attitude.

What part of the museum makes everyone sneeze? The sta-tues.

What did the baker say when she won an award? It was a piece of cake.

Why couldn't the couple respond right away when looking at wedding venues? They were engaged.

What's Marco's favorite clothing store? Polo.

What do you call it when a lawyer takes a test early in the morning? A breakfast bar.

What do frogs use to track their exercise? Fit(rib)bits.

Where was the dripping coming from in the fridge? The leeks.

Why was the hockey player gifted a new cap? He was known for his hat tricks.

What vegetable is kind to everyone? The sweet potato.

How was the handsome runner described? Dashing.

What animals are the best to call if you get locked out of your house? Monkeys.

What did the geometry teacher say when the class had trouble solving a problem? Let's try a different angle.

Why don't phones ever go hungry? They have plenty of apps to choose from.

Why couldn't the family leave the room after playing with Legos? They were blocked.

What makes a basketball court trendy and accessorized? The hoops.

What did the sapphire's best friend tell her? You're a real gem.

Not to brag but I defeated our local chess champion in less than five moves. Finally, my high school karate lessons paid off.

Why is it a bad idea to iron your four-leaf clover? Cause you shouldn't press your luck.

I spent a lot of time, money, and effort childproofing my house… but the kids still get in.

When I was a kid, my mother told me I could be anyone I wanted to be. Turns out, identity theft is a crime.

Why do you never see elephants hiding in trees? Because they're so good at it!

A guy goes to his doctor because he can see into the future. The doctor asks him, "How long have you suffered from that condition?" The guy tells him, "Since next Monday."

What do you call a mac-n-cheese that gets all up in your face? Too close for comfort food.

Last night I had a dream that I weighed less than a thousandth of a gram. I was like, 0mg.

A cheese factory exploded in France. Da brie is everywhere!

I was really angry at my friend Mark for stealing my dictionary. I told him, "Mark, my words!"

I'm starting a new dating service in Prague. It's called Czech-Mate.

I was just reminiscing about the beautiful herb garden I had when I was growing up. Good thymes.

Why do dogs float in water? Because they are good buoys.

What do you call a shoe made of a banana? A slipper!

My wife said I was immature. So I told her to get out of my fort.

What's the tallest building in the world? The library, it's got the most stories.

What do Santa's elves listen to when they work? Wrap music.

Did you hear about the bacon cheeseburger who couldn't stop telling jokes? It was on a roll.

What do you call it when Dwayne Johnson buys a cutting tool? Rock pay-for scissors.

RAD DAD JOKES

If towels could tell jokes, I think they'd have a very dry sense of humor.

I slept like a log last night. Woke up in the fireplace!

I used to run a dating service for chickens. But I was struggling to make hens meet.

Why couldn't the green pepper practice archery? Because it didn't habanero.

Why did the stadium get so hot after the game? Because all the fans left.

Within minutes, the detectives knew what the murder weapon was. It was a briefcase.

I used to work in a shoe-recycling shop. It was sole destroying!

I thought about going on an all-almond diet, but that's just nuts!

So a vowel saves another vowel's life. The other vowel says, "Aye E! I owe you!"

My uncle named his dogs Rolex and Timex. They're his watch dogs!

Two goldfish are in a tank. One says to the other, "Do you know how to drive this thing?"

What do you call a donkey with only three legs? A wonkey!

A woman is on trial for beating her husband to death with his guitar collection. The judge asks her, "First offender?" She says, "No, first a Gibson! Then a Fender!"

I accidentally dropped my pillow on the floor. I think it has a concushion.

To the person who stole my place in line, I'm after you now.

St. Francis worked at Krispy Kreme. He was a deep friar.

In America, using the metric system can get you in legal trouble. In fact, if you sneer at any other method of measuring liquids, you may be held in contempt of quart.

I found a wooden shoe in my toilet today. It was clogged.

Some people can't distinguish between etymology and entomology. They bug me in ways I can't put into words.

I hate it when people say age is only a number. Age is clearly a word.

Did you hear about the ATM that got addicted to money? It suffered from withdrawals.

I'm reading a horror story in braille. Something bad is going to happen, I can just feel it.

My doctor told me I was going deaf. The news was hard for me to hear.

Which days are the strongest? Saturday and Sunday. The rest are weekdays.

If an English teacher is convicted of a crime and doesn't complete the sentence, is that a fragment?

Which U.S. state is famous for its extra-small soft drinks? Minnesota!

I got a hen to regularly count her own eggs. She's a real mathamachicken!

What did the Ranch say when someone opened the refrigerator door? "Close the door, I'm dressing!"

My wife asked me to get six cans of Sprite from the grocery store. I realized when I got home that I had picked 7Up.

Why do trees seem suspicious on sunny days? They just seem a little shady.

I don't really call for funerals that start before noon. I guess I'm just not a mourning person.

One of my favorite memories as a kid was when my brothers used to put me inside a tire and roll me down a hill. They were Goodyears.

I'm addicted to collecting vintage Beatles albums. I need Help!

I have a joke about chemistry, but I don't think it'll get a reaction.

What do you call an ant that has been shunned by his community? A socially dissed ant.

A Vicks VapoRub truck overturned on the highway this morning. Amazingly, there was no congestion for eight hours!

I don't trust stairs. They are always up to something.

How many narcissists does it take to screw in a light bulb? One. The narcissist holds the light bulb while the rest of the world revolves around him.

How many DIY buffs does it take to change a light bulb? One, but it takes two weeks and four trips to the hardware store.

How many paranoids does it take to change a light bulb? Who wants to know?

I read that by law you must turn on your headlights when it's raining in Sweden, but how am I supposed to know when it's raining in Sweden?

What did one plate say to another plate? Tonight, dinner's on me.

What's the most popular fish in the ocean? A starfish.

When I was a kid, my dad got fired from his job as a road worker for theft. I refused to believe he could do such a thing, but when I got home, the signs were all there.

Why didn't Han Solo enjoy his steak dinner? It was Chewie.

Why don't pirates take a bath before they walk the plank? They just wash up on shore.

I TRY NOT TO LAUGH AT MY OWN JOKES... *But we all know I'm hilarious!*

Did you hear about the racing snail who got rid of his shell? He thought it would make him faster, but it just made him sluggish.

RAD DAD JOKES

A turtle is crossing the road when he's mugged by two snails. When the police ask him what happened, the shaken turtle replies, "I don't know. It all happened so fast."

Did you hear about the guy who froze to death at the drive-in? He went to see Closed for the Winter.

I had a happy childhood. My dad used to put me in tires and roll me down hills. Those were Goodyears.

I know a bunch of good jokes about umbrellas, but they usually go over people's heads.

The bank keeps calling me to give me compliments. They say I have an outstanding balance.

What's a vampire's favorite ship? A blood vessel.

RAD DAD JOKES

Did you hear about the surgeon who enjoyed performing quick surgeries on insects? He did one on the fly.

There's only one thing I can't deal with, and that's a deck of cards glued together.

The past, the present, and the future walked into a bar. It was tense.

Knock knock.
Who's there?
Alabama.
Anybody with you?
Nope, I'm Alabama self.

Daughter: I have a lot of friends named Nathan. There's Nathan Miller, Nathan Radcliff, Nathan Lewis.
Me: When they are together, do you call them the United Nathans?

RAD DAD JOKES

What's the least-spoken language in the world? Sign language.

What do you call a hippie's wife? Mississippi.

I searched for a lighter on Amazon, but all I could find were 6,000 matches.

Did you hear about the shepherd who drove his sheep through town and was given a ticket for making an ewe turn.

Did you hear about the cat who ate a ball of yarn? She had mittens.

Did you hear they arrested the devil? Yeah, they got him on possession.

A friend of mine didn't pay his exorcist. He got repossessed.

How do you tell the difference between an alligator and a crocodile? You will see one later and one in a while.

What happens when it rains cats and dogs? You have to be careful not to step in a poodle.

What do you call 50 pigs and 50 deer? 100 sows and bucks.

Why do cows wear bells? Because their horns don't work.

What do you call a fish with no eye? A fsh.

Son: Dad, I'm hungry.
Dad: Hi hungry, I'm Dad.

Police arrested a bottle of water because it was wanted in three different states: solid, liquid, and gas.

What do you call a lazy kangaroo? Pouch potato.

Why is grass so dangerous? Because it's full of blades.

What's the Easter bunny's favorite type of music? Hip-hop.

A friend of mine is known for sweeping girls off their feet. He's an extremely aggressive janitor.

I'm an expert at picking leaves and heating them in water. It's my special tea.

RAD DAD JOKES

My son's fourth birthday was today. When he came to see me, I didn't recognize him at first. I had never seen him be four.

I recently went to the "World's Tiniest Wind Turbine" exhibit. Honestly, not a big fan.

I was out on a walk when I saw a sign that said, "Man wanted for robbery." I went in and applied for the job.

How long should socks be? Twelve inches, so you can fit in one foot.

Did you hear the joke about experiencing déjà vu? Did you hear the joke about experiencing déjà vu?

Dad: Did you hear about the kidnapping at school?
Son: No. What happened?
Dad: The teacher woke him up.

A bartender broke up with her boyfriend, but he kept asking her for another shot.

I'm reading a novel where the main character has strained the muscles around his spine. That's his back story.

My doctor told me I have really grown as a person. Well, her exact words were that I gained excess weight.

What do you call someone who always states the obvious? Someone who always states the obvious.

Scientists have discovered what is believed to be the world's largest bedsheet. More on this story as it unfolds.

You can't plant flowers if you haven't botany.

What did the French chef give his wife for Valentine's Day? A hug and a quiche.

A couple of cups of yogurt walk into a country club. "We don't serve your kind here," the bartender says. "Why not?" one yogurt asks. "We're cultured."

A pirate walks into a bar with a paper towel on his head. The bartender says, "What's with the paper towel?" The pirate says, "Arrr! I have got a Bounty on me head!"

What did one DNA say to the other DNA? Do these genes make me look fat?

It's a shame that the Beatles didn't make the submarine in that song green. That would've been sublime.

Did you hear the one about the kid who started a business tying shoelaces on the playground? It was a knot-for-profit.

A guy walks into a bar, and there's a horse serving drinks. The horse asks, "What are you staring at? Haven't you ever seen a horse tending bar before?" The guy says, "It's not that. I just never thought the parrot would sell the place."

Why did Beethoven get rid of his chickens? All they said was, "Bach, Bach, Bach…"

Do I enjoy making courthouse puns? Guilty.

What do you need to make a small fortune on Wall Street? A large fortune.

How does the man in the moon get his hair cut? Eclipse it.

Teacher: "There are two words I don't allow in my class. One is gross, and the other is cool."
Johnny: "So, what are the words?"

To the person who stole my bed, I won't rest until I find you.

Why should you never mention the number 288? It's too gross.

What does a mobster buried in cement soon become? A hardened criminal.

Why was the pig covered in ink? Because it lived in a pen.

Did you hear about the guy who stole 50 cartons of hand sanitizer? They couldn't prosecute—his hands were clean.

RAD DAD JOKES

Why was the rookie police officer assigned to hunt the cannibal? The more seasoned officers had already been eaten.

What do you call a snitching scientist? A lab rat.

What's the difference between a man wearing pajamas on a bicycle and a guy wearing a tuxedo on a unicycle? Attire.

Did you hear about the aquatic sea mammals that escaped from the zoo? It was otter chaos.

What did the skeleton order with its beer? A mop.

Why do nurses like red crayons? Sometimes they have to draw blood.

How much do I love crunchy tacos? From my head tomatoes.

RAD DAD JOKES

My IQ test results came back. They were negative.

If athletes get athlete's foot, what do astronauts get? Missile toe.

My wife asked me to sync her phone, so I threw it into the ocean.

What did one cannibal say to the other while they were eating a clown? Does this taste funny to you?

What's a bad wizard's favorite computer program? Spell check.

In a freak accident today, a photographer was killed when a huge lump of cheddar landed on him. To be fair, the people who were being photographed did try to warn him.

Not sure if you have noticed, but I love bad puns. That's just how eye roll.

Why do pumpkins sit on porches? They have no hands to knock on the door.

My friend wants to become an archaeologist, but I'm trying to put him off. I'm convinced his life will be in ruins.

I got hit in the head with a can of Coke today. Don't worry, I'm not hurt. It was a soft drink.

Cooking out this weekend? Don't forget the pickle. It's kind of a big dill.

A steak pun is a rare medium done well.

Why did the raisin go out with the prune? Because he couldn't find a date. I had a date last night. It was perfect. Tomorrow, I'll try a grape.

How many mystery writers does it take to change a light bulb? Two: One to screw it in most of the way and another to give it a surprise twist at the end.

My dentist offered me dentures for only a dollar. It sounded like a good deal at the time, but now I have buck teeth.

I have been breeding racing deer. Just trying to make a quick buck.

I'm reading a book about anti-gravity. It's impossible to put down!

It hurts me to say this, but I have a sore throat.

I know a surgeon who puts organs back in upside down. I told him that's not funny, but he said it was an inside joke.

My girlfriend says it's either her or my career as a news reporter. I have some breaking news for her.

Inflation is really getting out of hand, but that's just my five cents.

When a woman is giving birth, she is literally kidding.

A termite walks into a bar and asks, "Is the bar tender here?"

Why did the crab never share? Because he's shellfish.

What did the guy say when he arrived in Antarctica? Well, that wasn't a warm welcome.

My friend keeps saying "Cheer up, man. It could be worse. You could be stuck underground in a hole full of water." I know he means well.

Dad: I was just listening to the radio on my way into town and apparently an actress just killed herself.

RAD DAD JOKES

Mom: Oh my! Who!?
Dad: Uh, I can't remember. I think her name was Reese something.
Mom: WITHERSPOON!?!?
Dad: No, it was with a knife.

A slice of apple pie is $2.50 in Jamaica and $3.00 in the Bahamas. These are the pie rates of the Caribbean.

My wife tried to unlatch our daughter's car seat with one hand and said, "How do one-armed mothers do it?" Without missing a beat I replied, "Single handedly."

Mom: How do I look?
Dad: With your eyes.

Today I heard YouTube, Twitter, and Facebook are all merging. They're going to call it You-Twit-Face.

RAD DAD JOKES

Server: Sorry about your wait.
Dad: Are you saying I'm fat?

What has two butts and kills people? An assassin.

What did the pirate say on his 80th birthday?
AYE MATEY!

If Snoop Dogg dies before pot becomes legal in the US, he will be rolling in his grave.

Kid: Hey, I was thinking…
Dad: I thought I smelled something burning.

Knock knock.
Who's there?
Nobel.
Nobel who?
No-bel, so I just knocked.

What do you call a cow with two legs? Lean beef.

What do you call a cow with no legs? Ground beef.

First you Russian...then European...then Finnish.

I just watched a documentary about beavers. It was the best dam show I ever saw!

Where did the college-aged vampire like to shop? Forever 21.

What did the horse say after it tripped? "Help! I have fallen and I can't giddy up!"

Do you know what the loudest pet you can get is? A trumpet.

Why wasn't the woman happy with the Velcro she bought? It was a total rip off.

RAD DAD JOKES

Waitress: "Soup or salad?"
Dad: "I don't want a SUPER salad, I want a regular salad."

What do you get when you cross a snowman with a vampire? Frostbite.

What does an angry pepper do? It gets jalapeño your face.

As a lumberjack, I know that I have cut exactly 2,417 trees. I know because every time I cut one, I keep a log.

Want to hear a joke about a piece of paper? Never mind, it's tearable.

Did you hear the one about the bed? No? That's because it hasn't been made up yet!

Why do chicken coops only have two doors? Because if they had four, they would be chicken sedans!

RAD DAD JOKES

I was interrogated over the theft of a cheese toast. Man, they really grilled me.

A three-legged dog walks into a bar and says to the bartender, "I'm looking for the man who shot my paw."

I had a dream that I was a muffler last night. I woke up exhausted!

You heard of that new band 1023MB? They're good but they haven't got a gig yet.

Time flies like an arrow. Fruit flies like a banana.

Did you hear about the guy who invented Lifesavers? They say he made a mint.

Did you see they made round bales of hay illegal in Wisconsin? It's because the cows weren't getting a square meal.

RAD DAD JOKES

Dad, to a singer: "Don't forget a bucket."
Singer: "Why?"
Dad: "To carry your tune."

What do you call a lonely cheese? Provolone.

I told my 14-year-old son I thought Fortnite was a stupid name for a computer game. I think it's just too weak.

How do you make a Kleenex dance? Put a little boogie in it!

How do you tell the difference between a frog and a horny toad? A frog says, "Ribbit, ribbit" and a horny toad says, "Rub it, rub it."

What do prisoners use to call each other? Cell phones.

Why did the Clydesdale give the pony a glass of water? Because he was a little horse!

RAD DAD JOKES

What do you call a fish with two knees? A "two-knee" fish.

Your mom and I let astrology get between us. It just Taurus apart.

A guy walked into a bar and lost the limbo contest.

Two peanuts went walking down the street. One was assaulted.

Mom said I should do lunges to stay in shape. That would be a big step forward.

Mom texted me from the grocery store to say they're out of pasta, and we're penneless.

Justice is a dish best served cold. If it were served warm, it would be just water.

Most people can't tell the difference between entomology and etymology. I can't find the words for how much this bugs me.

Mom asked me to put ketchup on the grocery list. Now I can't see anything.

A magician was walking down the street — then he turned into a store.

We're renovating the house, and the first floor is going great, but the second floor is another story.

At first, I thought my chiropractor wasn't any good, but now I stand corrected.

My boss asked me why I only get sick on workdays. I said it must be my weekend immune system.

RAD DAD JOKES

Every night, I have a tough time remembering something, but then it dawns on me.

I can tolerate algebra, maybe even a little calculus but geometry is where I draw the line.

I was going on an expensive vacation with a classical pianist, but he was too baroque.

My therapist told me I have problems expressing my emotions. Can't say I'm surprised.

If money doesn't grow on trees, then why do banks have branches?

I just paid $100 for a belt that doesn't fit. What a huge waist!

I finally watched that documentary on clocks. It was about time.

Can anyone tell me what oblivious means because I have no idea.

Why can't you send a duck to space? Because the bill would be astronomical.

What side of a tree grows the most branches? The outside!

What happened when the world's tongue-twister champion got arrested? They gave him a tough sentence.

What do you call a boomerang that doesn't come back? A stick.

What breed of dog can jump higher than a skyscraper? Any breed of dog. Skyscrapers can't jump.

Why did the computer get mad at the printer? Because it didn't like its toner voice.

RAD DAD JOKES

Why did the broom decide to go to bed? It was very sweepy.

Did you hear about the square that got into a car accident? Yeah, now he's a rect-angle!

How do you tell the difference between a bull and a cow? It's either one or the utter.

Why can't you ever run through a campsite? You can only ran — it's always past tents.

Why don't astronomers like Orion's Belt? It's a big waist of space.

What's the easiest way to burn 1,000 calories? Leave the pizza in the oven.

What did the photon say to the hotel bellhop? No luggage, I'm traveling light.

RAD DAD JOKES

What's the difference between a poorly dressed kid on a bicycle and a well-dressed kid on a tricycle? Attire!

Why is the cow always smiling? It's in a good mooood, I guess.

Why did the coffee go to the police? To report a mugging.

Did you hear about the king who was exactly 12 inches tall? He was a great ruler!

I never buy pre-shredded cheese. Because doing it yourself is grate.

What do scholars eat when they're hungry? Academia nuts.

I like telling Dad jokes…sometimes he laughs.